WHY DO I FEEL LIKE THIS?

SHINSUKE YOSHITAKE

There are lots of people in the world that I like.
But there are some people I don't like at ALL.

Some of them say mean things to me. Some of them make me annoyed. And some of them make me upset.

Sometimes I wish they'd trip over a rock and hurt themselves.

When people upset me, I start thinking about other things I don't like. My head gets full of grumpy thoughts like "Why is the world against me?" And that makes me even more upset!

Hating people doesn't feel good.

 This is what I imagine doing to people who annoy me.

 I shrink them till they're really tiny.

 Then I pick them up...

 and go SPLAT!

 I invent a remote-control robot. It sends out an invisible beam that gives them a tummy ache.

I get a pet wasp and train it to chase them away.

If I've had a bad day, I imagine all sorts of things.

I'm a film star and I'm acting in a very sad scene. I might even win an award for it!

When something sad happens, I win Sad Points. When I collect enough points, I can swap them for something I want!

Sometimes I try to make bad feelings go away by doing something completely different.

I put a box on my head and pull a face that nobody can see.

I roll up my socks into little balls.

I take the salad dressing out of the fridge and shake it really hard.

I collect all the spoons in the house and line them up.

I stick my head in my pillow and sing a song.

And sometimes I sing into my pillow and then have a nap.

Sometimes it helps to think about something else. Even small things can make me stop thinking about bad feelings.

"Wow! That sounds exciting. What was it like?"

"It's hard to describe. What could I compare it to?"

"Hmm..."

Perhaps I should try comparing my feelings to something? They're a bit like a sudden shower of rain. I can't do anything to stop it happening.

It's cold and horrible and everything feels like a mess!

If sad feelings are like rain, maybe it's best to find somewhere to hide until the rain goes away.

Perhaps I could build my own secret hiding place. That would be amazing!

Or maybe if there was only a little bit of rain,
I could lie down in it and try to enjoy it.

Either way, if sad feelings really are
like rain, they'll go away eventually.

I never know when sad things might happen. It would be great if I could cheer myself up whenever I wanted.

If I'm in a bad mood, sometimes having a bath makes me feel better. I wonder if that's because bad feelings are clinging to my body?

That might be why I can't see the fun things around me.

If that's true, I wonder if they fall off when I run or move around?

But even if my bad moods and sad feelings don't go away completely, I can still...

eat yummy food

talk to friends

or look at a pretty view.

Argh! He annoys me so much!

Hmm...

Yeah, I don't like him either.

I used to think that all grown-ups liked each other and everything was easy for them. But now I don't think that's true.

Even if I don't like someone at first, we might become friends one day. If we talk to each other, we can learn more about one another.

Sometimes I might think I don't like someone, but it's only because we disagree about something small.

But even so, there are still people I just don't get on with.

"READY...GO!"

Hmm, they're making their toys fight.

 Hey, wait a minute! Perhaps the people I don't like are being controlled by a monster?

Maybe the monster is out to get me?

Perhaps this is what happens.

1 The monster controls someone.

Maybe the monster gets paid every time it makes me feel a bad feeling? That's why it controls people!

The monster giggles when it watches sad films.

It always tries its best to do its worst.

It even tries to make the people I love feel bad!

What if it's true and there really IS a monster?

I hate that monster so much!

I don't want to make the monster happy. So when I feel sad, or when things are going wrong, I tell myself "Everything's going to be fine!"

Then I go and do something I enjoy.
And the monster won't get any money from me!

Monsters hate humming!

Every night I go to bed with a smile on my face.

It's because I'm thinking really hard about how I can make the monster have a terrible time.

When it hears people laughing, it trips over its own tail.

Whenever I make friends with someone nice, I say to them "Hey, let's hate the monster together!"

If we think up lots of fun things to do, the monster won't be able to make us sad!

But on some days, I think it helps to pretend that it does.

Even when we grow up, there will still be things that make us sad and people we don't like. But that's okay.

We can dwell on bad feelings, run away from them, or decide to face them. It's up to us to choose what to do.

I want to be someone who can do that.

Because I REALLY don't like that monster!

I'm home!

Translated from the Japanese

First published in the United Kingdom in 2020 by
Thames & Hudson Ltd, 181A High Holborn, London WC1V 7QX

Reprinted 2020, 2022, 2024

Original edition © 2019 Shinsuke Yoshitake / Bronze Publishing, Inc.
This edition © 2020 Thames & Hudson Ltd, London

All Rights Reserved. No part of this publication may be reproduced or transmitted in any form or by any means, electronic or mechanical, including photocopy, recording or any other information storage and retrieval system, without prior permission in writing from the publisher.

British Library Cataloguing-in-Publication Data
A catalogue record for this book is available from the British Library

ISBN 978-0-500-65232-9

Printed in China

Be the first to know about our new releases, exclusive content and author events by visiting
thamesandhudson.com
thamesandhudsonusa.com
thamesandhudson.com.au